Predator Face-Off

Melissa Stewart

NATIONAL GEOGRAPHIC

Washington, D.C.

For Laura, Kathryn, and Shelby, editors extraordinaire —M.S.

The author and publisher gratefully acknowledge the expert content review of this book by Bill Swanson, Ph.D., director of animal research, Center for Conservation and Research of Endangered Wildlife, Cincinnati Zoo, and the literacy review of this book by Mariam Jean Dreher, professor of reading education, University of Maryland, College Park.

Author's Note: All kinds of predators live on Earth. This book invites young readers to compare and contrast three predators that belong to different animal groups (fish, mammal, reptile), live in different environments (ocean, savanna, forest), and hunt in different ways.

The title page photo shows a great white shark coming out of the water. The photo on the Table of Contents page shows a king cobra with its hood extended. This makes the snake look bigger to its enemies.

Photo Credits:

AL: Alamy Stock Photo; GI: Getty Images; NPL: Nature Picture Library; SS: Shutterstock;

Cover (UP LE), vladoskan/Getty Images; header (throughout): (snake), HuHu/Shutterstock; (cheetah), Airin.dizain/Shutterstock; (shark), AKorolchuk/Shutterstock; vocabulary art (throughout), Ken Cook/Shutterstock; 1, Chris & Monique Fallows/NPL/Alamy Stock Photo; 3, Eric Isselée/Shutterstock; 4, Carlos Villoch - MagicSea.com/Alamy Stock Photo; 5 (UP), Stuart G Porter/Shutterstock; 5 (LO), Michael and Patricia Fogden/Minden Pictures; 6-7, wildestanimal/

Getty Images; 8-9, 3DMI/Shutterstock; 10 (UP), BW Folsom/Shutterstock; 10 (LO), Martin Prochazkacz/Shutterstock; 11, B Christopher/Alamy Stock Photo; 12-13, Andy Rouse/Nature Picture Library; 14-15, Eric Isselée/Shutterstock; 16, ZSSD/Minden Picturess; 17, Keith Lewis Hull England/Getty Images; 18, WaterFrame/Alamy Stock Photo; 19 (UP), Rodrigo Friscione/Alamy Stock Photo; 19 (CTR), Bertie Gregory/Nature Picture Library; 19 (LO), Anyka/Alamy Stock Photo; 20, Jim Cumming/Getty Images; 21, David Kleyn/Alamy Stock Photo; 22, Jim Cumming/Getty Images; 22-23, Patrick K. Campbell/Shutterstock; 24, Jim Cumming/Getty Images; 25, Robert Pickett/Alamy Stock Photo; 26 (UP), Matthijs Kuijpers/Alamy Stock Photo; 26 (LO), reptiles4all/Shutterstock; 27, Isselee/Dreamstime; 28, Mark Conlin/Alamy Stock Photo; 29, Kim Taylor/Getty Images; 30 (LE), Jeff Rotman/Getty Images; 30 (RT), Valdecasas/Shutterstock; 31 (UP LE), Elsa Hoffmann/Shutterstock; 31 (UP RT), Marcus Siebert/Alamy Stock Photo; 31 (LO LE), reptiles4all/Shutterstock; 31 (LO RT), Andre Coetzer/Shutterstock; 32 (UP LE), Jim Abernethy/Getty Images; 32 (UP RT), Federico Veronesi/Getty Images; 32 (LO LE), Zeeshan Mirza/Alamy Stock Photo; 32 (LO RT), reptiles4all/Shutterstock

Library of Congress Cataloging-in-Publication Data

Names: Stewart, Melissa, author.
Title: Predator face-off / Melissa Stewart.
Description: Washington, DC : National Geographic, [2017] | Series: National Geographic readers | Audience: Ages 4-6. | Audience: K to grade 3.
Identifiers: LCCN 2016051333 (print) | LCCN 2017009785 (ebook) | ISBN 9781426328114 (pbk. : alk. paper) | ISBN 9781426328121 (hardcover : alk. paper) | ISBN 9781426328138 (e-book) | ISBN 9781426328145 (e-book + audio)
Subjects: LCSH: Predatory animals--Juvenile literature. | Predation (Biology)--Juvenile literature.
Classification: LCC QL758 .S7425 2017 (print) | LCC QL758 (ebook) | DDC591.5/3--dc23
LC record available at https://lccn.loc.gov/2016051333

**National Geographic supports K–12 educators with ELA Common Core Resources.
Visit natgeoed.org/commoncore for more information.**

Printed in the United States of America
19/WOR/1

Table of Contents

What's a Predator?

Great white sharks swim in the sea. Cheetahs run across the land. Parrot snakes slide along tree branches.

They are very different. But they all eat meat.

These animals are predators (PRED-uh-ters).

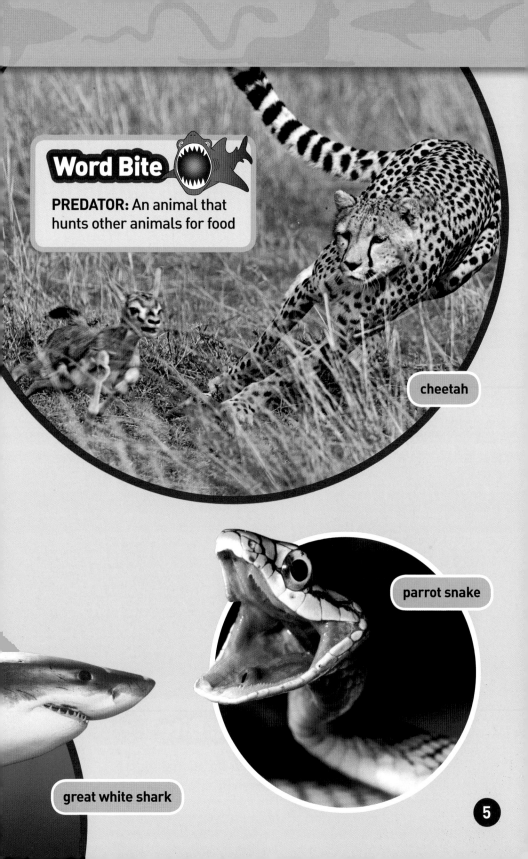

Word Bite

PREDATOR: An animal that hunts other animals for food

cheetah

parrot snake

great white shark

Shark Attack!

A great white shark spots a seal. It darts up and crashes into its prey. *Chomp!* The shark takes a big bite. It swims in a circle. Then it starts to eat.

Word Bite

PREY: An animal that is eaten by another animal

A great white shark is the size of a pickup truck. It's one of the biggest fish in the world. And its body is built to hunt.

TAIL: Pushes the shark through the water at up to 25 miles an hour

SKIN: Feels ripples when animals move in the water

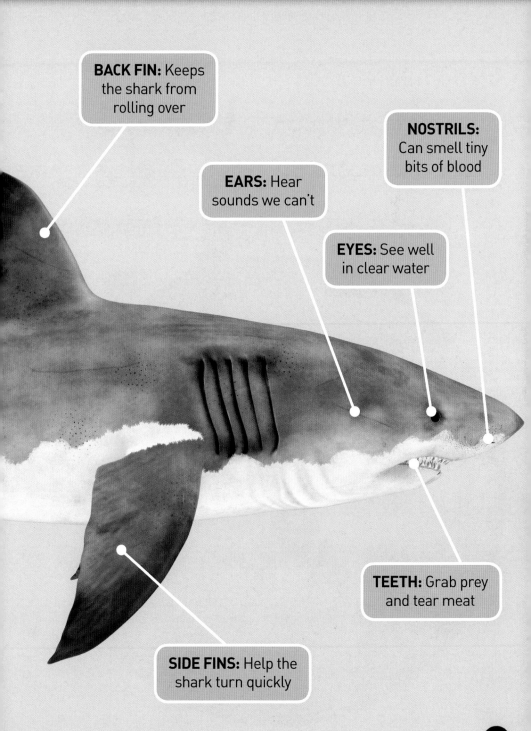

BACK FIN: Keeps the shark from rolling over

NOSTRILS: Can smell tiny bits of blood

EARS: Hear sounds we can't

EYES: See well in clear water

TEETH: Grab prey and tear meat

SIDE FINS: Help the shark turn quickly

How many teeth does a great white shark use at once? About 50.

shark teeth

Q What do you call the stuff stuck between a shark's teeth?

A Slow swimmers.

This photo shows the teeth and jaw on a great white shark skeleton.

Each tooth will wear out. Then the one behind it takes its place. A shark may use 20,000 teeth in its life.

Run, Cheetah, Run

Shh! A cheetah slinks through the grass. It creeps closer and closer to a gazelle (guh-ZELL).

The cheetah leaps. The chase is on!

Thud! The predator knocks the gazelle to the ground and bites its neck.

Time to eat.

13

Cheetahs are wild cats. They live in the grasslands of Africa.

How does a cheetah's body help it hunt? Take a look.

TAIL: Helps with balance during quick turns

EYES: See prey up to three miles away

EARS: Hear sounds we can't

BACK: Bends to help the cheetah run fast

TEETH: Bite and kill prey

LEGS: Pounce, run, and knock over prey

CLAWS: Grip the ground as the cheetah runs

Cheetahs are the fastest animals on land. They can run more than 60 miles an hour—but not for long.

They have to slow down after about 20 seconds.

The Need for Speed

Are cheetahs the only fast predators on Earth? No way! Lots of animals use speed to get food.

A mantis shrimp breaks open a clam shell with its claws. It can punch through water at 50 miles an hour.

A sailfish can swim up to 68 miles an hour. It uses its super speed to catch smaller fish.

A peregrine (PEAR-eh-gren) falcon dives to catch smaller birds. It can travel up to 200 miles an hour.

A chameleon (kuh-MEEL-yun) has a quick tongue. It can grab an insect faster than you can blink your eyes.

It's a Snake!

A parrot snake flicks its tongue.
In. Out. In. Out.

Finally, it picks up a scent. Tree frog!

The snake winds through the trees.
Then it spots the prey. It darts
forward and grabs the frog.

Dinnertime!

Q How are sharks and snakes the same?

A Both words have six letters.

21

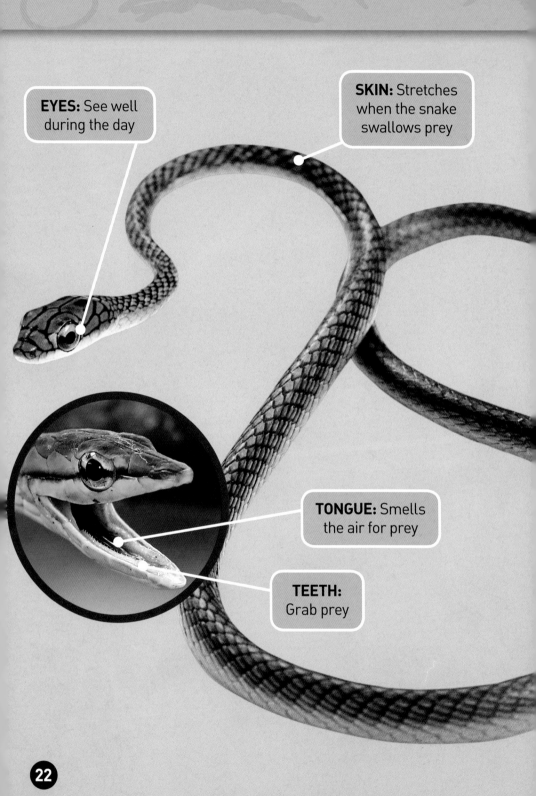

EYES: See well during the day

SKIN: Stretches when the snake swallows prey

TONGUE: Smells the air for prey

TEETH: Grab prey

THIN BODY: Doesn't get stuck on branches

The parrot snake lives in Central America and South America. It makes its home in forests. Its body is perfect for hunting in trees.

Word Bite

SCUTES: The wide scales on a snake's belly

SCUTES: Grip tree bark so the snake won't fall

A parrot snake has 36 small teeth. They can grab prey. But they can't chew.

How does the snake swallow prey?

1 It stretches its mouth over the prey.

 2 It pulls back the jaws on one side of its head.

3 It pulls back the jaws on the other side of its head.

 4 Slowly. Slowly. The prey slides into the snake's mouth and down its throat.

Snakes With Venom

The inland taipan has the deadliest venom. Just one drop can kill a person.

Most snakes hunt like a parrot snake. But some snakes make venom. It flows into prey through two large fangs.

The Great Lakes bush viper has huge fangs, but its venom isn't strong enough to kill a person.

fangs

The king cobra is the biggest snake with venom. It usually eats other snakes.

Word Bite

VENOM: A liquid that some snakes use to hurt or kill other animals

All Kinds of Predators

Sharks. Wild cats. Snakes.

They're just a few of the predators that share our world.

A sea star has strong legs. They can pry open a clam's shell. What a tasty treat!

It's easy to guess how a jumping spider catches its prey. Pounce!

Predators live in many different places. And they hunt in all kinds of ways.

What in the World?

These pictures show close-up views of predators. Use the hints below to figure out what's in the pictures.

Answers are on page 31.

1

HINT: It keeps a shark from rolling over.

2

HINT: A cheetah uses these to grip the ground.

Word Bank

peregrine falcon   back fin   fangs   claws   tongue   teeth

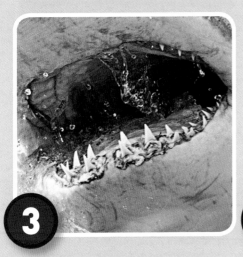

3

HINT: A shark uses 20,000 of these in its life.

4

HINT: This predator can dive 200 miles an hour.

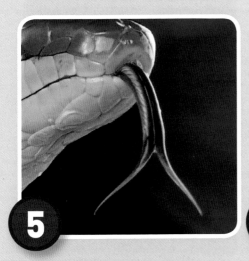

5

HINT: A snake uses it to smell.

6

HINT: Venom flows through these.

Answers: 1. back fin, 2. claws, 3. teeth, 4. peregrine falcon, 5. tongue, 6. fangs

PREDATOR: An animal that hunts other animals for food

PREY: An animal that is eaten by another animal

SCUTES: The wide scales on a snake's belly

VENOM: A liquid that some snakes use to hurt or kill other animals

Deadly Predators

Melissa Stewart

NATIONAL
GEOGRAPHIC

Washington, D.C.

For Tali, one of my favorite predators —M. S.

The publisher and author gratefully acknowledge the expert review of this book by Dr. Bill Swanson of the Cincinnati Zoo in Cincinnati, Ohio, U.S.A.

SECRET LIFE OF
PREDATORS
As seen on the National Geographic Channel

Design by YAY! Design

ISBN: 978-1-4263-1346-2 (Paperback)
ISBN: 978-1-4263-1347-9 (Library)

Photo credits

Cover (UP RT), PHOTO 24/Getty Images; 1, Sandy Flint/National Geographic Your Shot; 2, Kevin Horan/Getty Images; 4-5, Mark Stadsklev/Alaska Stock; 7 (UP), Hans Reinhard/Science Source; 7 (LO LE), Jim and Jamie Dutcher/National Geographic Image Collection; 7 (LO RT), Picture Press/Alamy Stock Photo; 8, James L Amos/Getty Images; 8-9, Martin Vavra/National Geographic Your Shot; 10, Paul Jarvis/National Geographic Your Shot; 11, Kathleen Reeder/National Geographic Your Shot; 12-13, Richard Ress/National Geographic Your Shot; 14, John Mitchell/Getty Images; 15 (UP), Dmitry Abezgauz/Shutterstock; 15 (CTR), Frans Lanting/Getty Images; 15 (LO), Giovanni Antonio Diaz/National Geographic Image Collection; 16, Mike Parry/Minden Pictures; 18 (INSET), Sue Flood/Minden Pictures; 18-19, Amos Nachoum; 20 (UP), Computer Earth/Shutterstock; 20 (UP CTR), Rob Wilson/Shutterstock; 20 (LO CTR), Maros Bauer/Shutterstock; 20 (LO), mallardg500/Getty Images; 21 (UP), Vincent Grafhorst/Foto Natura/Minden Pictures; 21 (CTR LE), risteski goce/Shutterstock; 21 (CTR RT), Walter Nussbaumer/National Geographic Your Shot; 21 (LO), Aimee Woodbury/National Geographic Your Shot; 22, Bianca Lavies/National Geographic Image Collection; 24, Thierry Lombry/National Geographic Your Shot; 26, Manny Ramirez/National Geographic Your Shot; 27, Austin Thomas/National Geographic Your Shot; 28-29, Anup Shah/Nature Picture Library; 30 (UP), Eduard Kyslynskyy/Shutterstock; 30 (CTR), AnetaPics/Shutterstock; 30 (LO), Ellen C/Shutterstock; 31 (4 UP LE), James L Amos/Getty Images; 31 (4 UP RT), Alex Wild/Getty Images; 31 (4 LO LE), mallardg500/Getty Images; 31 (4 LO RT), rujithai/Shutterstock; 31 (5), Simon Pidcock/National Geographic Your Shot; 31 (6 UP), Siddhardha Gargie/National Geographic Your Shot; 31 (6 LE), Paul Jarvis/National Geographic Your Shot; 31 (6 RT), Amos Nachoum; 31 (6 LO), skynetphoto/Shutterstock; 31 (7), Mike Parry/Minden Pictures; 32 (UP LE), Bianca Lavies/National Geographic Image Collection; 32 (UP RT), Kavun Kseniia/Shutterstock; 32 (CTR LE), Olga Selyutina/Shutterstock; 32 (CTR RT), EastVillage Images/Shutterstock; 32 (LO LE), Aimee Woodbury/National Geographic Your Shot; 32 (LO RT), Peter Ginter/Getty Images

**National Geographic supports K–12 educators with ELA Common Core Resources.
Visit natgeoed.org/commoncore for more information.**

Table of Contents

Hungry Hunters

Grizzly bears eat fish and other small animals. They usually weigh 300 to 500 pounds. The largest bears can weigh 800 pounds!

Wolves chase.
Sharks attack.
Bears lunge.

All these animals are predators. They're all after the same thing.

Meat. They need it to live and grow.

Word Bite
PREDATOR: An animal that hunts and eats other animals

Dogs in the Wild

Wolves are members of the dog family. So are foxes, coyotes, and African wild dogs. All of these dogs are powerful predators.

Big ears help wild dogs hear their prey. Sensitive noses help the dogs sniff out food.

Wild dogs also have large teeth and strong jaws. They can kill prey larger than themselves.

Word Bite
PREY: An animal that is eaten by another animal

A coyote has 42 teeth. Some can tear flesh. Others can crush bone.

African wild dogs hunt in packs.

An arctic fox stalks its prey.

Cats in the Wild

Thirty-six kinds of cats live in the wild. And they're all expert hunters.

The rusty-spotted cat is the smallest. It weighs less than a half-gallon jug of milk.

The rusty-spotted cat lives in India. At night, it hunts for birds, mice, lizards, and frogs.

Q What happened when the tiger swallowed a ball of yarn?

A It had mittens.

What is the biggest cat in the world? The Siberian tiger. It can weigh more than three large men.

Siberian tigers can eat up to 80 pounds of meat at one time.

Female lions hunt in a group. They work together to get a meal.

Most cats live alone. But lions live in a family group called a pride.

The males protect the group. The females do all the hunting.

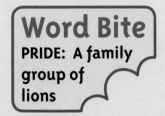
Word Bite
PRIDE: A family group of lions

A cougar has long, strong legs. But it can't run fast or far. It sneaks up on prey. Then it jumps on the animal and bites its neck.

Cougars have sharp teeth. They chop prey into bite-size bits.

Polar Power

The polar bear is the largest bear in the world. It's also the most deadly. Polar bears use their sharp teeth and huge paws to catch prey.

A polar bear has one of the world's best noses. It comes in handy when sniffing out dinner.

Q What do you call a polar bear with earmuffs?

A Whatever you want. It can't hear you!

They hunt alone. Polar bears mostly eat seals snatched from holes in the ice. But sometimes they eat small animals, too.

Mini-monsters

These predators may be small, but they sure are deadly!

Giant Water Bug
A giant water bug hunts fish and frogs, snakes and snails. It jabs prey with its mouthparts. Then it sucks out the animal's insides!

Wind Scorpion

This little critter has huge jaws and runs like the wind. It chases down termites, beetles, and even lizards. This one caught a cricket.

Short-tailed Shrew

This shrew's spit is full of venom. The shrew uses the spit to paralyze its prey.

Army Ants

A group of army ants looks like a moving carpet. The group can be as wide as a street. It can be as long as a football field. The ants kill and eat everything in their path.

Word Bite

PARALYZE: To make unable to move

VENOM: A liquid some animals make that is used to kill or paralyze other animals

15

Ocean Hunters

The great white shark can go weeks without eating. But when it gets hungry . . . look out!

The fierce fish has up to 3,000 teeth. It uses them to grab fish, seals, sea lions, and dolphins.

A great white shark attacks from below. It may push up with so much power that it rises out of the water.

Orcas attack a gray whale.

Orcas have two ways of hunting. They can surround a large animal and attack as a group. Then they share the meal.

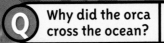
Orcas are called killer whales. Why? Because they eat all kinds of prey—birds, sea turtles, seals, and even sharks.

Orcas can also push a lot of fish into a tight ball. Then the orcas take turns eating the prey.

Super-predators

Biggest

A blue whale is longer than two school buses. But it eats shrimp-like critters no bigger than your pinky!

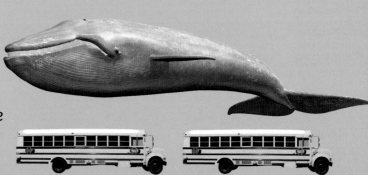

Fastest on Land

A cheetah can run as fast as a car on the highway. It's faster than any prey.

Fastest in the Air

How does a peregrine falcon catch prey? By diving through the air three times faster than a car on the highway.

Strangest

A fossa looks like a cross between a squirrel and a kitten. It hunts lemurs, birds, crabs, snakes, and more.

Longest Jumper

A cougar has powerful back legs. When it jumps from a high place, this big cat can jump the length of a pickup truck.

Most Beautiful

A sea anemone looks like a flower. But it has tentacles with venom. They can kill fish or shrimp in seconds.

Word Bite

TENTACLE: An arm-like part of an animal used to feel things or catch food

Snakes, Lizards, and Crocodiles

A black timber rattlesnake swallows a mouse.

Snakes kill their prey in different ways. Some snakes have venom in their fangs. The venom paralyzes the animals they catch. Then the snakes swallow the prey whole.

Other snakes don't use venom. The anaconda grabs an animal with its teeth. Then it curls around the prey and squeezes it to death.

Many lizards are small enough to sit in your hand. But the Komodo dragon is as big as a surfboard.

The giant lizard has 60 sharp, jagged teeth.

The Komodo dragon is the biggest lizard alive today. It eats birds, bird eggs, monkeys, wild boar, goats, deer, and more.

Q What do you get when you cross a kangaroo and a Komodo dragon?

A A leaping lizard.

Its spit is even
more deadly.
It's full of germs
that can kill prey
in one bite.

25

How does a hungry crocodile catch its prey? It lies in the water and waits. The patient hunter can wait for hours.

When prey passes by, the croc grabs it, pulls it underwater, and waits for it to drown.

What does a crocodile eat? Almost anything—fish, birds, snakes, deer, wildebeest (below), and more.

Perfect Predators

Crocs, cheetahs, wolves, sharks, and snakes are some of the most awesome predators on the planet.

But they don't hunt for fun.
They hunt to feed themselves
and their families.

Cheetahs are the
fastest animals
on land. They eat
animals such as
gazelles, impalas,
hares, and young
wildebeest.

Stump Your Parents

Can your parents answer these questions about predators? You might know more than they do!

Answers are at the bottom of page 31.

1

How much meat can some tigers eat at one time?

A. 10 pounds
B. 20 pounds
C. 40 pounds
D. 80 pounds

2

_____ are members of the dog family.

A. Wolves
B. Foxes
C. Coyotes
D. All of the above

3

Which kind of bear is the biggest in the world?

A. Brown bear
B. Black bear
C. Polar bear
D. Sun bear

4

Which predator sucks out the insides of its prey?

A. A rusty-spotted cat
B. A giant water bug
C. A peregrine falcon
D. A crocodile

5

Orcas are a kind of _____.

A. Fish
B. Whale
C. Insect
D. Reptile

6

Which of these animals does not hunt in groups?

A. Polar bear
B. Orca
C. Army ant
D. Lion

7

Which predator has the most teeth?

A. Gray wolf
B. Giant water bug
C. Great white shark
D. Komodo dragon

PARALYZE: To make unable to move

PREDATOR: An animal that hunts and eats other animals

PREY: An animal that is eaten by another animal

PRIDE: A family group of lions

TENTACLE: An arm-like part of an animal used to feel things or catch food

VENOM: A liquid some animals make that is used to kill or paralyze other animals

LEVEL
2

Alligators
and Crocodiles

Laura Marsh

NATIONAL GEOGRAPHIC

Washington, D.C.

For Izzy and Otto —L.F.M.

Copyright © 2015 National Geographic Society

Published by National Geographic Partners, LLC, Washington, D.C. 20036.

Paperback ISBN: 978-1-4263-1947-1
Reinforced Library Binding ISBN:
  978-1-4263-1948-8

Editor: Shelby Alinsky
Art Director: Amanda Larsen
Editorial: Snapdragon Books
Designer: YAY! Design
Photo Editor: Vanessa Mack
Production Assistants: Allie Allen, Sanjida Rashid

The publisher and author gratefully acknowledge the expert content review of this book by Kenneth L. Krysko, Ph.D., of the Florida Museum of Natural History, and the literacy review of this book by Mariam Jean Dreher, Professor of Reading Education at the University of Maryland, College Park.

Photo Credits
Cover (LO LE), Jim Brandenburg/Minden Pictures; header (throughout), dangdumrong/Shutterstock; vocab art (throughout), tapilipa/Shutterstock; 1, Jianan Yu/Reuters/Corbis; 3, Chris Parks/Image Quest Marine/Alamy Stock Photo; 4-5 (UP), John Kasawa/Shutterstock; 4-5 (LO), Eric Isselée/ Shutterstock; 6, Denton Rumsey/Shutterstock; 7, defpicture/Shutterstock; 9 (UP LE), TJUKTJUK/ Shutterstock; 9 (UP RT), Natali Glado/Shutterstock; 9 (LO), Steve Winter/National Geographic Image Collection; 10, PeterVrabel/Shutterstock; 11 (UP LE), prochasson frederic/Shutterstock; 11 (UP RT), Pete Oxford/Minden Pictures/Corbis; 11 (LO), C. Huetter/Alamy Stock Photo; 12-13, Mike Parry/ Minden Pictures; 14-15, Don Couch/Alamy Stock Photo; 16 (INSET), Joe & Mary Ann McDonald/ Alamy Stock Photo; 16-17, Mark Deeble and Victoria Stone/Getty Images; 18, Erich Schlegel/Corbis; 19, Andy Rouse/Nature Picture Library; 20 (UP), Becky Hale/NG Staff; 20 (LO), Matt Propert; 21 (UP), E.O./ Shutterstock; 21 (LO), Sorbis/Shutterstock; 21 (CTR LE), blickwinkel/Alamy Stock Photo; 21 (CTR RT), Victoria Stone & Mark Deeble/Getty Images; 22, Michael Runkel/Alamy Stock Photo; 23, Mike Parry/Minden Pictures; 24, Henry, P./Corbis; 25, Roger de la Harpe/Getty Images; 26, showcake/ Shutterstock; 27, Chris Johns/National Geographic Image Collection; 29 (INSET), WILDLIFE GmbH/ Alamy Stock Photo; 29, Doug Perrine/Nature Picture Library; 30 (UP), lluecke/iStockphoto; 30 (CTR), Joseph H. Bailey/National Geographic Image Collection; 30 (LO), niknikon/iStockphoto; 31 (UP LE), J. Gerard Sidaner/Science Source; 31 (UP RT), Brian J. Skerry/National Geographic Image Collection; 31 (LO LE), blickwinkel/Alamy Stock Photo; 31 (LO RT), clark42/iStockphoto; 32 (UP LE), WILDLIFE GmbH/Alamy Stock Photo; 32 (UP RT), showcake/Shutterstock; 32 (CTR LE), Joe & Mary Ann McDonald/Alamy Stock Photo; 32 (CTR RT), Natali Glado/Shutterstock; 32 (LO LE), lluecke/ iStockphoto; 32 (LO RT), defpicture/Shutterstock

National Geographic supports K–12 educators with ELA Common Core Resources. Visit natgeoed.org/commoncore for more information.

Table of Contents

Schneider's dwarf caiman

Guess What's Different

Snap! What big teeth you have!

Crocodiles and alligators look alike. They both have huge jaws with pointed teeth. They both have a long tail. Bumpy plates cover their bodies.

Can you tell which is the alligator and which is the crocodile?

But crocodiles and alligators are different. How can you tell them apart?

Alligators have a wide snout. It is rounded and U-shaped. Alligators are usually a dark color.

Croc Talk

SNOUT: an animal's nose and mouth that stick out from its face

Alligators usually live in freshwater.

dark in color

SNOUT

Crocodiles have a thinner snout. It is pointed and V-shaped. Crocodiles are lighter in color than alligators.

Crocodiles usually live in salt water.

lighter in color

SNOUT

7

A Pile of Reptiles

Though alligators and crocodiles are different, they are both reptiles. A reptile's body has scales or bony plates.

Snakes and lizards are reptiles with scales. Alligators and crocodiles are reptiles with bony plates called scutes (scoots). Both scales and scutes help protect reptiles' bodies.

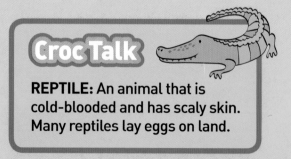

Croc Talk

REPTILE: An animal that is cold-blooded and has scaly skin. Many reptiles lay eggs on land.

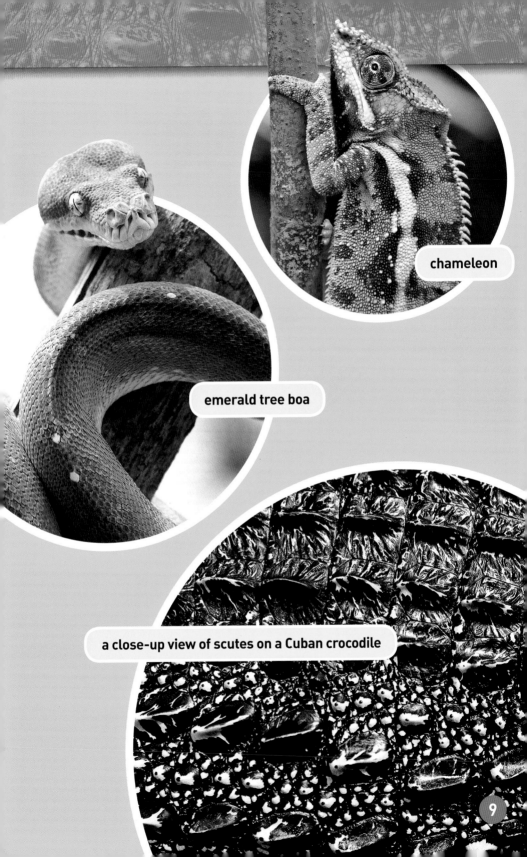

chameleon

emerald tree boa

a close-up view of scutes on a Cuban crocodile

9

Around the World

Alligators and crocodiles belong to a group of reptiles called crocodilians (krok-uh-DILL-ee-uns). There are 25 different kinds of crocodilians. They usually live in warm areas around the world.

Crocodilians are never far from the water. They spend a lot of time in ponds, lakes, marshes, wetlands, rivers, and swamps.

a gharial beside a lake

a broad-snouted caiman in a swamp

a slender-snouted crocodile in a river

Perfect for the Water

Alligators and crocodiles are built for living in the water. Both alligators and crocodiles have these parts.

EARS: Its ears are slits on its head. The slits close underwater.

NOSTRILS and **EYES:** Nostrils are on top of its snout. Eyes are on top of its head. A crocodilian can breathe and see while the rest of its body is underwater.

EYELIDS: Each eye has a top and a bottom eyelid. A third eyelid is clear. It protects the eye while underwater.

LUNGS: A crocodilian can hold its breath for up to two hours when its head is underwater.

TAIL: A strong tail pushes its big body through the water.

FEET: Its feet are webbed like flippers. They help a crocodilian swim quickly through the water.

BODY: It floats easily.

a young saltwater crocodile

American crocodiles

Crocodilians have excellent senses. They can see, smell, and hear better than many other reptiles. They see much better in the dark than we do.

Croc Talk

SENSES: sight, smell, hearing, taste, and touch

PREY: an animal that is eaten by another animal

Crocodilians have special skin, too. They can feel something moving nearby. In muddy water, they can easily find their prey.

Grabbing Dinner

Crocodilians are carnivores (CAR-nuh-vors), which means they eat meat. However, they are not picky eaters.

spectacled caiman

All kinds of fish, insects, birds, frogs, snakes, and mammals make a tasty meal. Even big animals such as antelope and buffalo are on the menu.

A Nile crocodile tries to grab a wildebeest from the herd.

American alligator

Alligators and crocodiles can go for months without eating. But when they're hungry, watch out!

A crocodilian waits for its prey to get close. Then it shoots out of the water and grabs the animal. Its big, strong jaws hold the prey underwater to drown it. Then the crocodilian gulps down dinner.

7 FUN FACTS
About Crocodilians

1 Alligator teeth are hollow.

There is only one place on Earth you can find both alligators and crocodiles in the wild—southern Florida, U.S.A.

2

ALABAMA GEORGIA

F L O R I D A

★Tallahassee

ATLANTIC OCEAN

GULF OF MEXICO

Tampa

Lake Okeechobee

West Palm Beach

Miami

The Everglades

Approximate range of the alligator in Florida

Approximate range of the American crocodile

0 100 miles
0 150 kilometers

Key West

Florida Keys

3

Crocodilians lose their teeth and get new ones all through their lives.

Crocodilians grow a lot. Newly hatched young are less than a foot long. But adults are 10 to 20 feet long!

4

5

Some crocodilians lay up to 90 eggs at one time. That's a lot of babies!

Mothers come running (or swimming!) when they hear their young call for help.

6

7

Like lions, crocodilians can roar.

King of the Crocs

A saltwater crocodile feeds in a sanctuary in Australia.

The largest crocodilian is the saltwater crocodile. It can grow to more than 20 feet long  and weigh over 2,200 pounds. It is an excellent swimmer and can travel far out to sea.

Saltwater crocodiles may be the most dangerous crocodilians of all. They are most likely to attack—and they are deadly!

Nest and Nursery

Most reptiles lay their eggs and leave. But crocodilians stick around. They stay close to the nest and protect their young.

Some kinds of crocodilians build a mound of plants, mud, and leaves for a nest.

Other kinds of crocodilians
dig a hole for a nest.

Crocodilian babies hatch
from their eggs.

A mother crocodilian waits for a
few months. When she hears squeaks
from the eggs, she uncovers the nest.
The eggs begin to hatch.

The mother gently carries the hatchlings in her mouth. She takes them to the water for their first swim. And they're off!

Croc Talk

HATCHLING: an animal that has just come out of its shell

American alligator

Endangered

New crocodilians hatch every year. But sometimes more animals die than hatch. Crocodilians can become endangered.

American alligators were once endangered. Then laws were made to protect them. Their numbers grew. Now there are over one million American alligators alive today.

Other crocodilians are now endangered. What can you do to help save these cool crocs and alligators?

The Morelet's crocodile, or Mexican crocodile, was once endangered. Now it is listed as of "least concern."

The most endangered species is the Philippine (FILL-ih-peen) crocodile. There are only about 250 left in the wild.

Croc Talk

ENDANGERED: at risk of dying out completely

QUIZ WHIZ

How much do you know about crocodilians? After reading this book, probably a lot! Take this quiz and find out.

Answers are at the bottom of page 31.

How many different types of crocodilians are there?

A. 4
B. 12
C. 17
D. 25

Alligators have a _____-shaped snout.

A. square
B. U
C. V
D. heart

Which of these is the largest?

A. the saltwater crocodile
B. the Nile crocodile
C. the American alligator
D. the Philippine crocodile

4

Baby crocodilians hatch in a _____.

A. tree
B. pond
C. nest
D. river

5

Crocodilians lose their _____ and get new ones throughout their lives.

A. teeth
B. eyes
C. ears
D. tails

6

When does a mother crocodile uncover the eggs in the nest?

A. when the moon is full
B. when she hears squeaks
C. when she's hungry
D. when it's been exactly 30 days

Crocodiles and alligators eat _____.

A. birds
B. fish
C. some big animals
D. all of the above

7

ENDANGERED: at risk of dying out completely

HATCHLING: an animal that has just come out of its shell

PREY: an animal that is eaten by another animal

REPTILE: An animal that is cold-blooded and has scaly skin. Many reptiles lay eggs on land.

SENSES: sight, smell, hearing, taste, and touch

SNOUT: an animal's nose and mouth that stick out from its face

Deadliest Animals

Melissa Stewart

NATIONAL
GEOGRAPHIC

Washington, D.C.

For Colin
—M.S.

Paperback ISBN: 978-1-4263-0757-7
Library Edition ISBN: 978-1-4263-0758-4

Cover (LO RT), Karine Aigner/National Geographic Image Collection; 1, Ian Waldie/Getty Images; 2, Radius Images/Getty Images; 4 (UP), Gary Randall/Getty Images; 4 (CTR), Duncan Noakes/iStockphoto; 4 (LO), James Martin/Getty Images; 5, Stephen Robinson/NHPA/Photoshot; 6-7, Mitsuaki Iwago/Minden Pictures; 8, Gerry Pearce/Alamy Stock Photo; 9 (UP), DEA/Christian Ricci/De Agostini/Getty Images; 9 (LO), SA team/Foto Natura/Minden Pictures/National Geographic Image Collection; 10, Ira Block/National Geographic Image Collection; 11, Rinie Van Meurs/Minden Pictures; 13 (UP), Jason Edwards/National Geographic Image Collection; 13 (LO), Steve Turner/Oxford Scientific/Getty Images; 14, Beverly Joubert/National Geographic Image Collection; 15, Tim Fitzharris/Minden Pictures/National Geographic Image Collection; 16-17, Karl Ammann/Digital Vision/Getty Images; 18, Konrad Wothe/Minden Pictures/National Geographic Image Collection; 19, Frans Lanting; 20, DLILLC/Corbis; 21 (UP), John Pitcher/Design Pics/Corbis; 21 (CTR), Radius Images/Corbis; 21 (LO), Jack Goldfarb/Design Pics/Corbis; 22, Bates Littlehales/National Geographic Image Collection; 23 (UP), Deshakalyan Chowdhury/AFP/Getty Images; 23 (LO), George Grall/National Geographic Image Collection; 24, Armin Maywald/Foto Natura/Minden Pictures/National Geographic Image Collection; 25 (UP), Ho New/Tasmania Police/Reuters; 25 (LO), Ian Waldie/Getty Images; 26, Stephen Frink/Science Faction/Getty Images; 27, David Doubilet/National Geographic/Getty Images; 28, Cary Sol Wolinsky/National Geographic Image Collection; 29, Michael Melford/National Geographic Image Collection; 30 (UP LE), Martin Harvey/Gallo Images/Getty Images; 30 (UP RT), Panoramic Images/Getty Images; 30 (CTR LE), Andrew Holt/Photographer's Choice/Getty Images; 30 (CTR RT), Brian Skerry/National Geographic Image Collection; 30 (LO LE), Gary Vestal/Riser/Getty Images; 30 (LO RT), Paul Zahl/National Geographic Image Collection; 31 (UP LE), James Forte/National Geographic Image Collection; 31 (UP RT), Andrew Bannister/Gallo Images/Getty Images; 31 (CTR LE), David B. Fleetham; 31 (CTR RT), Lius Angel Espinoza/National Geographic Your Shot; 31 (LO), Heidi & Hans-Juergen Koch/Minden Pictures/Getty Images; 32-33, Gary Bell/Oceanwide Images; 33 (RT), Viorika Prikhodko/iStockphoto; 34, Shane Drew/iStockphoto; 34-35, Fred Bavendam/Minden Pictures/National Geographic Image Collection; 35 (INSET), Hal Beral/VWPics/SuperStock; 36, Mark Moffett/Minden Pictures; 37 (UP), ZSSD/Minden Pictures/National Geographic Image Collection; 37 (CTR), Mark Moffett/Minden Pictures/National Geographic Image Collection; 37 (LO), Mark Moffett/Minden Pictures/Getty Images; 38, Scott Leslie/Minden Pictures/National Geographic Image Collection; 39, Zheng Jiayu/XinHua/Xinhua Press/Corbis; 40, IMAGEMORE Co., Ltd./Getty Images; 41, Mark Moffett/Minden Pictures/Getty Images; 42, David Maitland/Photoshot; 43, Ian Waldie/Getty Images; 44, David Scharf/Science Faction/Getty Images; 45, Mitsuhiko Imamori/Minden Pictures/National Geographic Image Collection; 46 (UP), Karen Mower/iStockphoto; 46 (CTR LE), Gary Bell/Oceanwide Images; 46 (CTR RT), David Doubilet/National Geographic/Getty Images; 46 (LO LE), Keren Su/The Image Bank/Getty Images; 46 (LO RT), Ira Block/National Geographic Image Collection; 47 (UP LE), Armin Maywald/Foto Naturs/Minden Pictures/National Geographic Image Collection; 47 (UP RT), Johan Swanepoel/iStockphoto; 47 (CTR LE), Scott Leslie/Minden Pictures/National Geographic Image Collection; 47 (CTR RT), Mark Moffett/Minden Pictures/Getty Images; 47 (LO LE), ZSSD/Minden Pictures/National Geographic Image Collection; 47 (LO RT), Deshakalyan Chowdhury/AFP/Getty Images

**National Geographic supports K–12 educators with ELA Common Core Resources.
Visit natgeoed.org/commoncore for more information.**

Table of Contents

Deadly Surprises

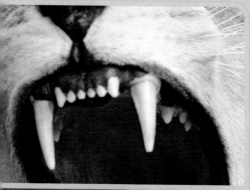

Huge teeth?
Check.

Razor-sharp claws?
Check.

Fast and fierce?
Check.

The African lion has all the features you'd expect to find in one of the world's deadliest animals. These powerful predators are skillful stalkers that usually hunt together in groups called "prides" and can take down prey ten times their size. That's why people often call lions "the kings of the jungle."

But are lions the deadliest
animals of all?

Not quite.

Lions certainly score high on the deadliest list, but they don't take the number one spot. And if you think all of Earth's most dangerous creatures are big, fierce hunters, you're in for some surprises.

Surprise 1:

Some deadly animals eat only plants.

Red kangaroos spend their days quietly nibbling on grasses, but when they feel threatened, watch out! A hard kick in the chest can break a person's ribs and collapse the lungs.

Surprise 2:

Some deadly animals are smaller than the palm of your hand.

Oak processionary (sounds like PRO-seh-shen-ary) caterpillars are only 2 inches long, but beware of their hairy bristles. They can cause rashes, asthma attacks, and even deadly allergic reactions.

DEADLY DEFINITIONS

ALLERGIC: When the body responds to something with a rash, breathing trouble, or even death

VENOM: A poisonous liquid inside some animals' bodies

Surprise 3:

Some deadly animals may be closer than you think.

Rattlesnakes live throughout the United States, and they bite about 8,000 people each year. Even though rattlesnake venom is deadly, most people get treated quickly and survive.

Mighty Hunters

Polar Bears

The polar bear is the largest land predator alive today. Like a lion, a polar bear is a skilled hunter that knows exactly when and how to attack.

The clever carnivore looks for a hole in the ice and waits. When a seal comes up for air, the polar bear pounces and grabs the seal with its sharp teeth.

DEADLY DEFINITIONS

CARNIVORE: An animal that eats the meat of other animals

11

Saltwater Crocodiles

Saltwater crocodiles are just as fierce as polar bears—and just as patient, too.

Lurking below the water's surface, a croc lies in wait for its prey. When an unsuspecting animal passes by, the 1,000-pound beast explodes out of the water, grabs its victim, and drags it under the water to drown. Yikes!

DEADLY DEFINITIONS

PREY: An animal that is eaten by other animals

Crocodile Safety

DANGER

Crocodiles inhabit this area.
Attacks cause injury or death.

– Keep away from the water's edge.
– Do not enter the water.

– Do not clean fish near the water's edge.
– Remove all fish and food waste.

Death Toll

The saltwater crocodile is the most deadly large predator. It can easily take down a water buffalo and has even been known to kill sharks off the coast of Australia.

Big and Brutal

Hippopotamuses

Hippopotamuses are usually gentle giants. During the day, they lounge and snooze in shallow water holes. At night, they lumber onto land and munch on grasses and leaves.

But if a boat gets between a hippo and the deep water or between a mother and her calf, the animal will panic. It may tip over the boat and attack the passengers with its powerful jaws.

weird but true

A hippo can outrun you on land and outswim you in the water. You don't stand a chance against an angry hippo!

Elephants

Like hippos, elephants are usually calm, peaceful animals. But when an elephant feels threatened, it will attack.

The huge herbivore can stab enemies with its tusks and crush them with its feet. Sometimes it grabs an attacker with its trunk and tosses the possible threat into the air.

Elephants are the largest animals on land, so they can do a lot of damage.

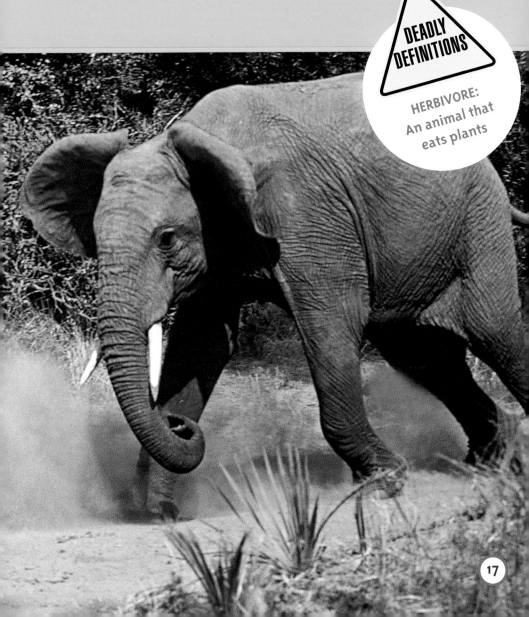

DEADLY DEFINITIONS

HERBIVORE: An animal that eats plants

Cape Buffaloes

Large herds of Cape buffaloes graze hour after hour on thick grasses. It might seem like they're focusing on their food, but they're also on the lookout for danger.

Death Toll

In Africa, Cape buffaloes are known as "black death" due to their dark color and ferocious nature.

When these huge, hulking animals feel angry or scared, they charge at enemies with their heads down. Often they charge together as a group. A stampede of Cape buffaloes can kill predators quickly with their sharp hooves and hooked horns.

Scary Snakes

About 3,000 species of snakes live on Earth, and most of them make venom. Snakes use venom to kill prey and protect themselves from enemies.

DEADLY DEFINITIONS

SPECIES: A group of similar creatures that can mate and produce healthy young

TOXIC: Poisonous, capable of causing injury or death

Most snakes are too small or too shy to attack humans. But about 300 species can kill a person who's in the wrong place at the wrong time.

Golden Eyelash Viper

Green Pit Viper

☠ Toxic Tidbit

The Indian cobra's venom isn't as toxic as the venom of some other snakes, but it often lives close to people and that makes it a major threat. Indian cobra bites kill thousands of people each year in Asia.

Red-diamond Rattlesnake

Which snake is the deadliest of all?

That's a hard question to answer.

Hook-nosed Sea Snake

This fish-hunting reptile lives in coastal waters and has the most poisonous venom of any snake. Just one drop can kill a person. Like other snakes, it has lungs and breathes air, but it can stay underwater for up to five hours.

Russell's Viper

This snake lives in rice paddies and grassy areas of Asia and may bite farmers. Its venom isn't quite as toxic as the hook-nosed sea snake's venom, but it has more toxin in its body. That means it delivers more venom in each bite.

Black Mamba

Other snakes may have stronger venom, but the black mamba moves fast and isn't afraid to attack. When an enemy gets too close, the black mamba raises its head high and hisses. If the predator doesn't back off, the snake strikes again and again.

Ferocious Fish

Great White Shark

The great white shark is the largest meat-eating fish in the ocean. The sight of its huge mouth and 3,000 jagged teeth would send shivers up anyone's spine.

What makes this shark so dangerous? Its super senses. It hears well and has excellent eyesight. Most important, its sense of smell is 10,000 times better than ours.

weird but true

A great white shark can smell tiny amounts of blood in the water up to 3 miles away.

Stonefish

Stonefish are masters of disguise.
Instead of swimming in search of
food, they blend into their rocky
surroundings and wait for prey to pass by.

If a hungry predator grabs a stonefish—
or a person accidentally steps on one—
thirteen spiky spines deliver a painful blast

of venom. The
wound swells, the
victim's muscles feel
weak, and the area
becomes paralyzed.
If the person isn't
treated, he or she
could die.

Puffer Fish

When an enemy attacks, a puffer fish gulps water and blows up like a prickly balloon. But that's not the fish's only trick for protection.

If a predator manages to take a bite of a puffer fish, it gets a mouthful of nasty-tasting toxin. Yuck!

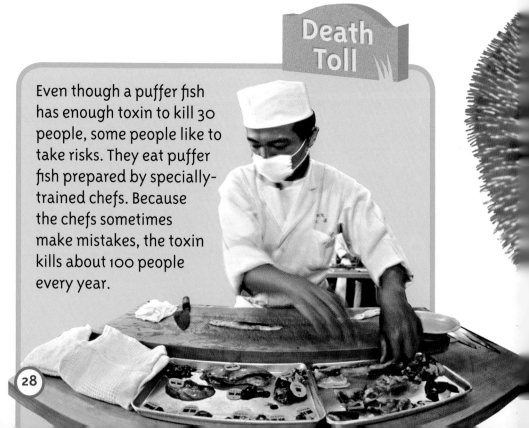

Death Toll

Even though a puffer fish has enough toxin to kill 30 people, some people like to take risks. They eat puffer fish prepared by specially-trained chefs. Because the chefs sometimes make mistakes, the toxin kills about 100 people every year.

10 Cool Things About Deadly Animals

1 Female lions do most of the hunting, but male lions always eat first.

2 On hot, sunny days, a crocodile pants like a dog to stay cool.

3 Most young fish are called fingerlings, but young sharks are called pups.

4 Baby hippopotamuses are born underwater.

5 If you shine a black light on a scorpion, it glows in the dark.

6

A jellyfish doesn't have a brain.

7

All snakes have teeth, but only snakes that make venom have fangs.

8

If an octopus loses an arm, another one will grow in its place.

9

Some poison dart frogs contain enough toxin to kill ten people.

10

A honeybee has five eyes—three small ones on top of its head and two large ones in front.

No Bones About It

Fish aren't the only sea creatures that can be hazardous to your health. Some ocean invertebrates can be just as deadly.

Box Jellyfish

You may have been stung by a jellyfish, but the box jellyfish is in a class by itself.

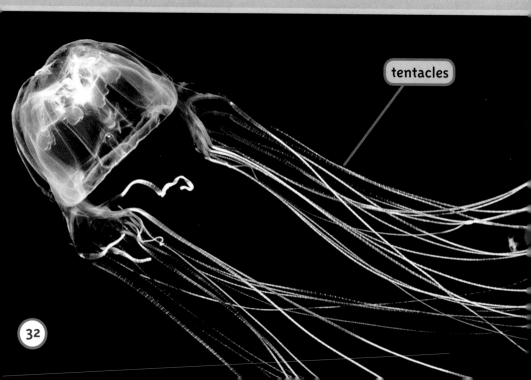

tentacles

Toxic Tidbit

A box jellyfish's body is the size of a basketball, but its tentacles can be up to 9 feet long.

Each of its tentacles has thousands of tiny stinging cells. Together, they pack enough toxins to kill 60 people, and death can come in just 4 minutes.

body

tentacles

DEADLY DEFINITIONS

INVERTEBRATE: An animal with no backbone

Blue-ringed Octopus

A blue-ringed octopus is the size of a golf ball, but it has a deadly bite.

Most of the time, the octopus uses its toxic saliva to catch crabs and shrimp. But its powerful poison can paralyze up to twenty people. Within minutes, anything that attacks this little octopus stops breathing and dies.

DANGER

BLUE RING OCTOPUS

A blue-ringed octopus's skin is usually yellowish brown. But bright-blue spots or rings suddenly appear when the octopus feels scared.

Small But Deadly

The ocean isn't the only place on
Earth with small, deadly creatures. They
also live in fields and forests, wetlands
and deserts.

Poison Dart Frogs

Scientists think that poison dart frogs eat toxic insects that make them deadly. Touch the slimy skin of these brightly-colored creatures and you could be dead in minutes.

☠ Toxic Tidbit

Some native rain forest peoples catch poison dart frogs, collect their venom, and rub it on darts they use to hunt. That's how the frogs got their name.

Honeybees

Honeybees help us by pollinating many of our favorite fruits, vegetables, and nuts. But they can also be deadly.

About 1 in 4,000 people is severely allergic to bee venom and can die after just one sting if left untreated. But all the toxin from a stinging swarm of angry bees can kill anyone.

DEADLY DEFINITIONS

POLLINATE: To transfer pollen from one flower to another, allowing plants to make fruit and seeds

What happened when the honeybee called its hive?

A It got a buzzy signal.

weird but true

Bee bearding is the practice of attracting bees to the human body by hanging the queen from the chin.

39

Scorpions

A scorpion's huge, claw-like pincers are its weapon of choice. But if a predator attacks or its prey puts up a fight … ZAP! A swift strike with the stinger on its tail usually does the trick.

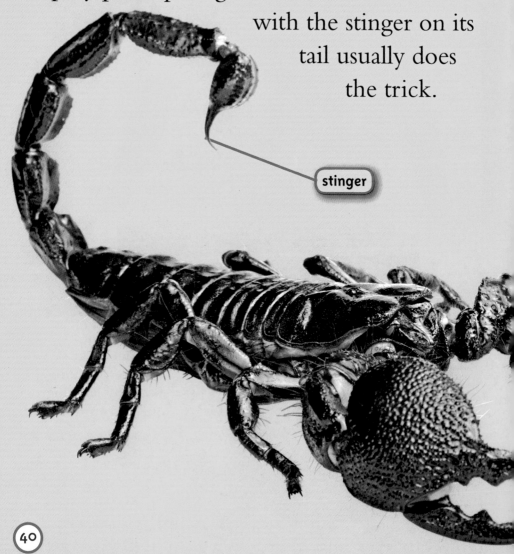

stinger

The stinger contains a hollow tube connected to two sacs full of venom. The scorpion controls the amount of venom its stinger delivers, so bigger victims get a bigger dose.

Death Toll

Of the nearly 2,000 scorpion species alive today, only 30 or 40 have venom strong enough to kill humans. Still, thousands of people die each year from scorpion stings.

Sydney Funnel Web Spider

Small and shiny. Dark and deadly. That's how people in Australia describe the Sydney funnel web spider.

Most of the time, this spider uses its sharp fangs and deadly venom to catch insects and other prey. But if a person gets too close, the spider won't hesitate to bite.

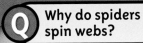

☠ Toxic Tidbit

Scientists developed medicine to protect people from Sydney funnel web spider venom in 1981. No one has died from its bite since.

Deadliest of All

So what's the deadliest animal of all?

The mosquito—that pesky little insect with the whiny hum!

Mosquitoes carry some of the worst diseases on Earth, including malaria and West Nile virus. And when a mosquito sucks blood from an animal, germs can enter the victim's body. That's why it's a good idea to use bug spray when there are insects around.

From tiny mosquitoes to gigantic elephants, the world's deadliest animals come in all sizes and shapes. And they live in every habitat you can think of. But each of them has a special way of keeping themselves safe in a dangerous world.

Glossary

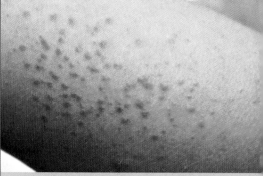

ALLERGIC: When the body responds to something with a rash, breathing trouble, or even death

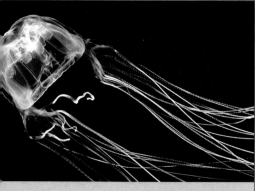

INVERTEBRATE: An animal with no backbone

PARALYZED: Unable to move

PREDATOR: An animal that hunts and eats other animals

SPECIES: A group of similar creatures that can mate and produce healthy young

CARNIVORE: An animal that eats the meat of other animals

HERBIVORE: An animal that eats plants

POLLINATE: To transfer pollen from one flower to another, allowing plants to make fruit and seeds

PREY: An animal that is eaten by other animals

TOXIC: Poisonous, capable of causing injury or death. A toxic substance is called a toxin.

VENOM: A poisonous liquid inside some animals' bodies

Index